101 Quotes

FOR THE CONSCIOUS MIND

MW00723294

DARREN MITCHELL

Scripture quotations are from the ESV® Bible (The Holy Bible, English Standard Version®), copyright © 2001 by Crossway, a publishing ministry of Good News Publishers. Used by permission. All rights reserved.

Every reasonable effort to attribute each quote to the original author has been made.

ISBN: 13: 978-1-7328104-2-6

This book was printed in the United States of America
To order additional copies of this book contact:
LaBoo Publishing Enterprise, LLC
staff@laboopublishing.com
www.laboopublishing.com

Acknowledgement

To my good friend and sister in Christ, Tamlyn Franklin, thank you for giving me the idea and inspiration to write this book. I had no intention of writing, but I'm glad I did.

Introduction

I love quotes. One quote at the right time can literally change a person's life. I think we forget sometimes just how powerful words can be. Not me though. Most of the quotes I chose came from my social media pages where I post quotes almost daily. Quotes to me aren't merely words on a page but principles that I live by. The quotes you read may land a bit differently for you and that's OK. That just goes to show how alive words really are. You and I can read the same exact thing but take away two completely different perspectives. I've taken the liberty to share how each quote has affected me or simply what I think about what was said. I hope that through my explanation, interpretation, or experience you will find something transformational. I mean, what good is a personal development book if it doesn't transform your life in even the most minute way? My desire is for something to touch you, so your life will forever be changed much how mine has. I believe we were all created to first grow and then share our experiences. I urge you to take what you can from this little book of quotes, grow from it, and then share it with those who you care for most.

101 Quotes

FOR THE CONSCIOUS MIND

1

Don't bother just to be better than your contemporaries or predecessors.
Try to be better than yourself.

~William Faulkner~

They say comparison is the thief of all joy. I've spent an entire lifetime comparing myself to my peers and those who are younger than I am and thinking that where they were was at least where I should be. That only breeds anger and resentment towards others. Comparing ourselves to others robs us of our peace. We must remember that each of us is on separate paths dictated by the choices we make. The key to improvement is not through comparison to others but striving to be better than you were yesterday, every single day.

2

A man who chases two rabbits

catches neither.

~Chinese Proverb~

If you're like me, everything seems to catch your eye. You can't seem to find your niche because you like so many things. One minute you're doing this and the next minute you're doing that. Your friends can never keep up with what business venture you're trying this month. However, here's the thing: though you may be a jack-of-all-trades, you're really a master of none. One key to life is having the ability to focus on one thing at a time. Chase more than one rabbit and go hungry, chase one rabbit at a time, and you'll always have something to eat.

3

Care about what other people think and
you will always be their prisoner.

~Lao Tzu~

How many dreams are deferred out of fear of what other people will say or think? How long are you going to remain trapped by what others see for you? For years, I had a burning desire to inspire and motivate people. However, I was trapped by what I thought people would think of me. Who will take me seriously? They'll laugh at me. No one cares what I have to say. These were just some of the thoughts I had that prevented me from moving forward with my dreams. How long will you remain a prisoner to someone else's thoughts?

4

The greatest danger for most of us lies not in setting our aim too high and falling short but in setting our aim too low and achieving the mark.

~ Michelangelo ~

We often hear how fear and self-doubt stop us from reaching our full potential. Heck, fear stops us from reaching for anything at all most of the time. However, fear can be more conspicuous at times. If we're not careful, fear will cause us to lead comfortable lives that on the surface appear to be great, but we're left with an inner turmoil without knowing why. Although we may have advanced in our careers or even accomplished a great deal, for most of us the level of fulfillment we're seeking isn't there. Why? Because deep down we know we aren't aiming high enough. We set the bar low enough to hit and feel good for a moment, but it never lasts. Fear hides behind mediocrity. The only way to combat it is to set BIG audacious goals! Goals so high they scare us. You'll be surprised at what happens once you set your sights on the stars.

5

*You can have anything you want
if you are prepared to pay for it.*

~ Unknown ~

Many of us have had some sort of health or weight loss goal in our lifetime. It always starts the same way: you're super excited about changing your lifestyle and eating habits. You save your favorite fitness model as your screensaver to remind you of the shape you're about to be in. You even consider paying for a gym membership. But once you get started, you quickly calculate the cost of having that amazing body and something in you says it is no longer worth it. This is life though. The question will remain the same: what is it worth to you? For any goal or dream, one must consider what they're willing to pay to receive it.

6

Your playing small does not serve the world.

~Marianne Williamson~

Do you get the feeling that there's more to you than what you show the world? Do you know you could be doing so much more, but you're afraid? Not afraid that you'll fail but that if you gave it 110 percent you'd be a force to be reckoned with. There's one thing stopping you though. If you become a success, what about everyone else? They'd be left behind. They'd be intimidated by your sheer presence, right? WRONG! The right people will be inspired by you. The world awaits your gifts and talents. It's not something to be hidden and ashamed of. They're to be embraced and shared with anyone secure enough in their own being to receive them. Never ever dumb yourself down to make others feel smart.

7

Change your habits. Change your life.

~ Unknown ~

Success leaves clues just look at any successful person. I'm not talking about the millionaires and billionaires we read about in magazines or watch on television but your grandparents who've been together for 30+ years, your cousin who's in amazing shape, or your aunt and uncle who are the most frugal people you've ever met and yet they secretly are millionaires. If you pay close enough attention, you'll see a common thread between them. It's in what they did every single day that made all the difference in what they've become. Not happy with where your life is headed? Change your habits. Oh, and guess what? It doesn't have to be major. It's the little changes that equal BIG results over time.

8

Dreams don't work unless you do.

~John C. Maxwell~

It's so easy to lie in bed all day hoping, dreaming, and wishing. A dream doesn't make a dream come true. The bible says that faith without works is dead. Therefore, dreams without action remain dreams. The way you manifest your dreams into reality is by physically working on them. Dreams are pulled from the ether onto the physical plain only by what you do. That's it.

9

*I'd rather attempt to do something great
and fail than to attempt to do
nothing and succeed.*

~Robert H. Schuller~

During the Olympics, many people from across the globe compete at a super high level to bring home that prized gold medal. Millions more watch from the comfort of their homes as athletes take huge leaps only to come crashing down in utter defeat. We criticize and may even laugh, but we're at home and they're the ones out there trying. They are failing big because they attempted something great. If only more of us had the courage to attempt something great. Sadly, most of us will attempt to do nothing and become very successful at it.

10

As a single footstep will not make a path on the earth, so a single thought will not make a pathway in the mind. To make a deep physical path, we walk again and again. To make a deep mental path, we must think over and over the kind of thoughts we wish to dominate our lives.

~Henry David Thoreau~

The Grand Canyon wasn't formed in a day. It was formed from a river flowing through it over millions of years. Isn't it amazing how some seemingly harmless water could have powered through an enormous rock and forged a 277-mile-deep path in it? That's the power of persistence. Our thoughts are no different. We think our thoughts are harmless so we pay no attention to them. All the while, they're flowing through our heads our entire lives, forging a mile-deep path in our mind which then shapes our thinking. Our thinking then shapes our lives. Can you see how important it is to not only pay attention to every thought that enters the mind but also immediately dismiss any thought that does not empower you?

11

Learn to be alone and to like it.
There is nothing more freeing and empowering
than learning to like your own company.

~Mandy Hale~

I remember the first time I went off on my own. I took a weekend trip about four hours away from home. I think the only way to really get to know yourself is to spend ample time alone. That weekend I learned about anxieties and insecurities I never knew existed, I guess because they were hidden behind the company of others like family, friends, and loved ones. You have a way of masking who you really are when you're with others. We put a mask on depending on how we want to be perceived. Without the protection of other people, you're left exposed with no mask on. However, when you learn to love and appreciate that person, real empowerment happens, and freedom is discovered. Try it. You might find that you prefer your OWN company to that of many people in your life right now.

12

You'll NEVER feel like it. If you only acted on what you felt like doing, can you imagine how uninspiring your life would be?

~Darren Mitchell~

This is a lesson I learned from waking up Monday-Friday at 3:30 in the morning. I do this not because I must be at work that early. But instead, to make it to the gym by 4:30am. Why in the world would a person wake up that early to work out? Well, because I know what it takes from me, mentally, to do something that insane. Do I ever feel like waking up that early? No, of course not! That habit thing is a complete myth. Even after waking up for 21 days straight, I still don't feel like doing it. I think it's actually the mundane tasks that are the most habit-forming. For an example, when and how you brush your teeth, which route you take to work, or what foot you put out first when taking the stairs. Everything else we want to do will always have an easier alternative that requires us to do nothing. Not eating healthy will ALWAYS be easier than choosing a salad. Staying home in bed will ALWAYS be easier than going to the gym, watching TV will ALWAYS be easier than sitting down to write a book. Does that mean we succumb to our feelings? Do we only do the things we absolutely feel like doing? Take a moment to imagine a life where you ONLY did the things you felt like doing...

13

Without counsel, plans fail,
but with many advisers, they succeed.

~Proverbs 15:22~

It is currently popular to be in search of a mentor or coach. To be honest, I believe they are necessary to succeed in life. A person can travel but so far on his/her own. If you never sought-after wise counsel, you would only know what you know. What we don't always consider are the many counselors and advisers we have at our disposal, whom, by the way, we use on a regular basis, never giving much thought to the pivotal role they have played in our lives. What successful person on this planet can say they've made it to where they are without the help of anyone?

14

Learn to see the blessing in your struggles.
Without them, you wouldn't be
where you are.

~Darren Mitchell~

Every hardship you've experienced, every struggle, and every failed business idea and even relationship, believe it or not, has made you the person you are today. In life, there are no losses. Only lessons. No matter how costly the lesson was, it was still a lesson. Many of my lessons landed me in jail. In the moment, I could only see the pain in it. Some of my struggles sent me into bankruptcy. I lost numerous cars, friends, and boatloads of money. ALL I now see as a blessing. I'm able now to not be ashamed of what I've been through but appreciate it. Without the countless lessons I've learned in life, I would not be this adamant about personal development. Without a mindset of personal development, you'll die. I am blessed to have gone through what I went through, I came up with few bumps and bruises and am now able to be an inspiration to many.

15

Successful people do what unsuccessful people are not willing to do. Don't wish it were easier; wish you were better.

~Jim Rohn~

At some point in their lives, successful people realized that to separate themselves from everyone else, they had to do what no one else was willing to do. Stop following the crowd. If everyone is doing it, it must be easy. Everyone stays up late playing video games, partying, and lying on the couch eating potato chips. Everyone is spending money recklessly pretending to be rich, but never knowing what real wealth feels like. The road to success isn't going to be easy. But never wish it were easy. Wish you were better.

16

Accept what is, let go of what was,
and have faith in what will be.

~ Unknown ~

Here's the interesting thing I have found about life. Whenever we experience anger, frustration, or anxiety, at its source, is non-acceptance. There is something about the present situation that we are failing to accept. If we are scheduled to give a speech and we become a nervous wreck, there can only be a few causes for this. We're fearful of messing up in some form or fashion or we're afraid of embarrassment. By not accepting these as possibilities, we resist with all our might only calling forth the thing we fear most. Remember what we resist persists. Freedom is found in accepting what is. What is only exist in your mind. As for the future, it is filled with infinite possibilities, so have faith in that.

17

If you have hope you have everything.

~Panda Express~

Though anything is possible. Why fixate on problems that can't be solved, situations that cannot be changed or issues you can do nothing about. Focusing on how much money you don't have won't create more money. Focusing on the love you do not have, will not bring love into your life. However, it is with hope that all our desires are made possible. All the thought leaders of old had one thing in common, a hope for a brighter future. Most of which, never lived to see it. But some did. I can't imagine a world without hope where everyone on the planet has given up. If I had not had even an ounce of hope while I was going through the toughest of times, I wouldn't be here today. Never give up hope.

18

The only limits that exist are the limits we place on ourselves.

~Darren Mitchell~

I hear so many people complain about their current circumstances and don't get me wrong, I've found myself complaining at times too. However, to add insult to injury, not only do we complain, but we make excuses too. I didn't come from a rich family, that person is smarter than I am, stronger than I am, has better genetics, grew up with both parents, and the list goes on. A person with two parents will complain about how hard life is and the person with one parent will say, "Hmph, lucky you." Meanwhile, the person who grew up in an orphanage will say, "At least you had one parent, I have no one." Then the person in the wheelchair will say, "Well at least you can walk, look at me!" However, the person in the grave isn't talking at all. Every day we see people in worse situations, with less time, less talent, and fewer resources doing the impossible. The only real limits we have are the ones we create in our minds.

19

When thinking about life remember this:
No amount of guilt can solve the past and
no amount of anxiety can change the future.

~ Unknown ~

Remaining fully present is the key to living a joyous and prosperous life. We have things in our past that we're not proud of. We all at times worry about the future. But all we really have is right now. Everything else is either being created (the future) in our minds or held (the past) in our minds. Either way, anything outside of the present moment is a figment of our imagination. Think about this for a sec. Can you change the past? Can you change the future? Change can only happen in the present moment.

20

*Become so free that no one
has access to your well-being.*

~Darren Mitchell~

Free yourself from the judgment of others. That doesn't mean people won't judge you. They will. It's OK, it doesn't have to affect you. Free yourself from comparing yourself to others. That doesn't mean people won't surpass you in life. But be OK with where you are in this moment. Free yourself from self-doubt. That doesn't mean you know everything in every situation. But know that you can figure it out. Know that you can speak with the right person, be in the right place, or learn what you don't know. With this knowledge, what can you do?

21

The question is not 'What if I die tomorrow?'
It is, 'What if I live another 20 or
30 years the way I am?'

~ Kim Wolinski ~

To get caught up in, "What if I die tomorrow?" and not think about what would happen if I lived another 20 years is futile. We often take for granted how long we've been on top of this earth. Just think, if you're 20 years or older, what would have happened if five years ago you decided to live the next five years to your fullest potential not leaving one stone left unturned and maximizing your time energy and resources. What if, five years ago, you planned to be alive for the next five years and decided to make major changes in your life. Where would you be? Life is a dance between knowing you might not be here tomorrow but planning to be around for the next 20 years. From that perspective, you should be asking, "How can I expand or grow?" The person you are right now won't get you to the person you want to become next week.

22

Challenge every thought that enters your mind.
Most people never question their own thinking.

~Darren Mitchell~

I hear we think anywhere between 50 and 60 thousand thoughts per day. Not only are most of these thoughts negative (about 80 percent), but most of these thoughts go unchecked, left in our brains to wreak havoc on our subconscious. Whenever a thought seeps into our subconscious, it becomes a part of our being. We begin to think that this is who we are. When I decided I wanted to write a book, naturally hundreds of thoughts sprung up telling me it was impossible like: "you'll never finish it, you don't finish anything," "you're not a writer, your English is terrible," and "why write it when it won't sell and if it does it'll never be a best seller so why bother?" How often do thoughts like these dominate your mind? My journey of self-improvement has led me to believe that it all starts in our minds. The successful individual can distinguish between what is real and what is a story in their head. The successful person can distinguish between what is possible and the voice in their brain trying to keep them safe. Because of this, most people will never achieve what they would call success. Challenge every single thought as if your life depends on it. Because it does.

23

What a wonderful life I've had!
I only wish I'd realized it sooner.

~Sidonie Gabrielle Colette~

When we were children, our only focus was on how much fun we could possibly have on any given day. We had nothing to worry about. Everything was taken care of. Play was our number one priority. Can you remember how much fun you used to have? However, something happens as we get older. We begin to focus on our future, bills, children of our own, and our careers. Fun gets replaced with worry. Suddenly we find ourselves miserable and depressed about the life we are living. Who wants to die miserable and depressed? Not me! It's important for us to keep a childlike mind. Be curious, ask questions, and have LOTS of fun! Stop taking yourself so seriously. The sooner you realize how wonderful life truly is, the longer you'll live. Don't wait until you're 65 to finally start living. Every moment you have breath in your lungs is a chance to live and to be happy.

24

The only people who don't make mistakes
are those who never try anything.

~Napoleon Hill~

Am I the only one who's afraid of making mistakes? Am I the only one afraid to try something new and exciting only to fall flat on my face? Is there something in life you've always wanted to do but never seemed to make it to or past the first step because fear paralyzed you? Well, you're not alone. Think about some of America's favorite brands. Each has had their fair share of failures along the way. Brands from Apple to Microsoft and McDonald's have released products that have failed miserably in the marketplace. Some product failures even cost the company hundreds of millions of dollars. Here's the funny thing: when you deliver value on a consistent basis, no one remembers your failures and when you're able to bounce back quickly from a setback, no one remembers it. However, there's only one sure-fire way to never ever make a mistake in life – never try anything at all.

25

We cannot teach people anything, we can only help them discover it within themselves.

~ Galileo ~

This is a personal favorite. Until I read this quote and studied the concept behind it, I used to want credit for everything I "taught" a person. If I shared some information, described, and walked you through an idea and you got it, I wanted credit for it. Then I learned, the only way for someone to learn something is that there must be something already in them that agrees on some level with what I'm telling them. God made us whole and complete from the very beginning. Everything we need to survive and thrive was implanted in us before we were born. It is through the guidance of elders who have trekked and navigated through life that we discover what is already in us. Can you imagine the life you speak into a young person speaking as if they already know and you just need to remind them?

26

Sometimes we stare so long at a door that is closing that we see too late the one that is open.

~Alexander Graham Bell~

To succeed in life, one must be able to adapt quickly. If you ever find yourself caught in quicksand, the way out is not by focusing on the sand below you. The way out of any problem isn't by focusing on the problem. If we stare at the problem, where will we find the solution? Staring at missed opportunities will only cause you to see missed opportunities. How depressing is that? Often, it's not that opportunities or open doors don't exist. We know that opportunities are all around us. Every day there is someone out there making their dreams come true. And nine out of 10 times they didn't have it any easier than we did. They simply decided to stare at the open doors that were around them.

27

I am the greatest.
I said that even before I knew I was.

~Muhammad Ali~

Many of us are familiar with the first sentence. When you read it, you can't help but hear Muhammad Ali's iconic voice saying, "I am the greatest." What's little known is that he said it to convince himself and then reassure himself that he was the greatest. There's a verse in the Bible that says, "Call forth the things which are not as though they were" (Romans 4: 17). This is what Muhammad Ali was doing. He called forth something that was not. He wasn't the greatest when he said he was the greatest. However, eventually, Muhammad Ali and "the greatest of all time" became synonymous. Speak to yourself what you could be, not what you are, and watch as you become that which you spoke of.

28

*If you think education
is expensive, try ignorance.*

~ Ben Franklin ~

Yes, it can get expensive to educate yourself whether you do it through formal schooling or on your own such as via certifications, books, workshops, and lectures. Ignorance, on the other hand, can get expensive too. Not knowing something on the job, could get you fired. Not knowing the tax code, could cost you thousands of dollars in taxes every year. Not knowing the laws of the state in which you live could cost you hundreds or even thousands of dollars in fines and court costs. Not knowing your mate or spouse, could cost you your relationship. You see where I'm going? The fundamental difference between the two is that education is an asset, while ignorance is a liability. What I mean is that no one can ever take away the knowledge that you gain through education. If you get fired from one place you can take your talents someplace else. Not to mention that education is an investment. Hopefully, the money you spend on education comes back to you in a form that is more valuable than what you paid for it. Ignorance, however, goes out and never comes back.

29

If it's not worth buying again.
Then it wasn't that valuable to begin with.

~Darren Mitchell~

I think about this every time I lose something—which is often. Most of the time, I never attempt to repurchase the item. I noticed that even when I thought something was my "favorite," after losing it, I realized it wasn't that valuable to me. Only the items that I HAD to have again really meant something to me. However, as I have matured in my wisdom, I realize that nothing material is that important anyway.

30

Don't chase people. Work hard and be yourself. Under these two principles, the right people will find their way into your life.

~ unknown ~

I get it, we're human. We are social creatures. There's something innate in every human being that has a need for acceptance. It only becomes a problem when that need for acceptance costs you your inner peace and happiness. To chase people, you must give up a little piece of yourself. Chase people long enough and you'll forget who you are. Instead, put your energy into something productive and work hard at it. Your satisfaction should come from the work that you do and the way you contribute to society. Just be yourself. I'd rather be liked for who I am than for who I'm not.

31

Successful people do what unsuccessful people are not willing to do even when it doesn't look like it makes any difference.

~Jeff Olsen~

I once heard that it takes 10 years to become an overnight success. To understand that concept you must have a particular mindset. Successful people understand this concept very well. Most unsuccessful people give up before they really give themselves a chance to succeed. If you look at the back-story of many famous names and businesses, you'll see a long trail of failures before hitting success. Wait a minute though; it's not always failures either but just plain old hard work. My favorite example of this is the motivational speaker, author, and preacher Eric Thomas. Most of us came to know him from his famous "Guru Speech." What most people don't realize is that he had been speaking for 10 plus years before that video broke and made him famous. This leads to another point. He obviously wasn't in it for the money, or else he would have quit a long time ago.

32

Never be a prisoner of your past.
It was just a lesson, not a life sentence.

~ Unknown ~

I've been through a lot in my past, but I've bounced back so hard nobody would ever know unless I told them. You don't have to look like what you've been through. The past is just that, the past. Your best bet is to leave it there. The only good use for your past is using it to propel you forward. There's always a way. You must train your mind to see opportunities and move fearlessly towards them.

33

It's your life.
No one is going to live it for you.

~Darren Mitchell~

First you must evaluate if your life is really your life or it was created for you? Did your parents tell you when you were younger what you were destined to be? Or are you living a life everyone expected you to live? Maybe they didn't tell you what to do but you felt pressured because of the expectation. You came into this world alone and you'll leave this world alone. It is your life. Figure out what you want to do with it. Your life depends on it.

34

*Happiness is not trying or finding,
it's deciding.*

~ Unknown ~

Happiness is an every month, week, or day decision. Why do I say that? Because we're too quick to make other people responsible for our OWN happiness. When someone says something we don't like, we're unhappy. If someone forgets to do something we like, we're unhappy. Then we say, "YOU made me this way." That is such a victim, powerless statement. All power is given up when you tell a person, "You made me…" Even the happiness you say you're searching for is only temporary and eventually leads to sadness and discontent. However, if you decide to be happy this will not only last but will be independent of anyone else.

35

When a flower doesn't bloom you fix the environment in which it grows, not the flower.

~ Alexander Den Heijer~

Now we're a little different than flowers, so it's important to work on ourselves. However, it's equally important to fix the environment in which we live. A flower will never grow in toxic soil. Much like the plant, neither will we. Toxic friends, toxic family, and even a toxic job can put an emotional strain on our well-being. The reason you aren't blooming is because you're still allowing weeds to grow in your garden. Your garden is your life. The only way to remove weeds from your life is by their roots or you must plant yourself in a new garden. The choice is yours.

36

Knowledge without practice is useless.

~Confucius~

The Bible puts this statement another way: "Faith without works is dead" (James 2: 26). In other words, nothing happens without action. I am a book junkie. I devour them like candy. It could even be considered an addiction. What I soon realized was that my addiction to knowledge and information was paralyzing me to act. I don't care how much you know, it means nothing until you're able to put it into practice. Then once you put it into practice, you must then practice it to perfect it. Don't get caught up in what I call positive procrastination. Procrastinating by doing something positive has no effect on the world in which you live. No number of books, audio programs, coaches, or seminars are going to do anything for you unless you do.

37

People would rather not hear about the
vision you have, because it reminds them
of the one they've lost.

~Jeff Olsen~

Have you ever shared a dream with someone with the biggest smile on your face? A dream that was so big, so exciting, that you couldn't contain yourself only to have the other person crack a half smile and an unenthusiastic, "Oh that's nice." Well, that's because simply having a dream reminds people of the ones they let go of or didn't have. Unfortunately, it is hard for a lot of people to celebrate the success in other people's lives when they've experienced nothing but failure. So, don't be discouraged by the lack of encouragement from others. You're on the right track.

38

Life changes, when you change your life.

~Darren Mitchell~

Life is simple. Well, it can be. We complicate life. Reality or life can bend to our will if we're willing to change. Everything that you have in your life is a result of the actions you decided to take. Life is the result of your actions. Therefore, to change your life you must change the actions you're taking. I remember when I finally decided that enough was enough. I was tired of getting into trouble. Tired of going to jail. And tired of being broke. I could have continued to blame those around me like my friends, parents, coworkers, etc. However, I realized none of them had the power to change my life so why focus on them anyway? Remember, it's always your fault no matter what. Why? Because you are the only one that has the power to change your life. So, for my life to begin to go in a different direction, I had to change course.

39

The journey of a thousand miles
starts with a single step.

~ Chinese Proverb ~

I think there are two lessons that are present with this one. The first being that every endeavor begins with the first step. The second is that no matter the size of the obstacle, or how far the road ahead may seem, it always breaks down to a single step. I think the hardest thing for most people to do is start. However, it makes sense. Usually starting is what takes up 80 percent of your energy. The rest you can leave to momentum or what author Darren Hardy calls The Big Mo. What am I trying to say? JUST START! Whatever it is just begin. Figure out the rest on the way to the top. I heard Dean Graziosi say, "Jump off the cliff and grow wings on the way down." It doesn't matter how big it seems or how far away it is. Somebody has what you want and guess how they got started? Yup, you guessed it, with the first step.

40

Courage is the commitment to begin,

without any guarantee of success.

~ Unknown ~

Courage is the number one quality I believe most people, including myself, are either missing or could certainly use more of. I was reading a book by author and real estate mogul Dean Graziosi called Millionaire Success and he has a chapter on the four levels of confidence. The first level of confidence is courage. Confidence is a knowing, a surety. However, it only comes through trial and error. To begin, it doesn't take confidence, but courage. Dean used an amazing example of courage in his book. He said to imagine that you were skydiving for the first time. You're standing at the threshold of the door leading to the outside world and all its vastness. You look out and see nothing but blue sky and clouds up above and thousands of feet below is the ground. Is it confidence that gets you to make the leap? It can't be as you've never done it before. There's no sure way to know that your parachute is going to deploy on time, or at all for that matter. The thing that will finally cause your feet to step out of that plane is courage.

41

When you can't change your situation,
change your perspective.

~Darren Mitchell~

There are certain things in life that simply can't be changed. You can't change who your parents are, who your siblings are, where you were born, your race, your height, and a whole host of other things. So, what do you do when you want something different but can't change the situation? You change your perspective. Changing your perspective means to see something with a different pair of eyes, not the ones you're currently using. One way to look at things is in worse case scenarios; not to be morbid or negative but to put what's really going on into perspective. Lost your car? Well, it could have been your home. Lost your home? Well, it could have been your life. Death is the great equalizer. You can't escape it. However, I've learned to use death to make *everything* else seem so insignificant. There's a funny cliché that was made famous in the movie *The Hangover:* after something serious happens to you just ask the question, "But did you die?"

42

Expect to win.

~Unknown~

Expectation is one big key to success. You get what you expect. People have been attracted to successful people since the beginning of time. It's well documented that there are certain characteristics that each and every successful person share. One of the characteristics is the mindset that they expect to win or succeed. Successful people have an unbelievable belief in themselves and the product or service they're selling. Expectation is a self-fulfilling prophecy. If you expect to lose, then you will naturally do things that will cause you to lose. In fact, when you expect to lose you don't even try, which of course leads to failure. Expecting to win, however, causes your brain to search for that outcome. You begin to ask yourself winning questions that lead to success. Expect to win, period.

43

Sacrifice is giving up something of a lower nature to gain something of a higher nature.

~Bob Proctor~

I began reflecting one day on where I was in life. I thought about my career, family, finances, health, and a bunch of other things. Then I began thinking about where I wanted to be in each of those areas. Here's what I realized: for me to go from where I was to where I wanted to be, I had to become a different person. I had to literally change who I was. Whoever I had been to get to that current state was not going to be enough to get me to the next level. Eric Thomas says it like this, "To be successful, you must be willing to, at any moment, sacrifice who you are, for what you will become."

44

Strive for progress, not perfection.

~ Unknown ~

I saw this quote in the gym and it immediately connected with me. If perfection is the goal, you'll never be happy. There isn't a perfect body, perfect relationship, and perfect way to be or act, there is no perfect anything. So, to chase perfection is to chase the ghost. The key to real happiness is progress. Watching yourself improve over time, over days, over weeks or months, and to be able to look back and see how far you've come, that's where the satisfaction comes in. You don't try to be perfect, you try to be better.

45

The greatest value in life is not what you get.
It's what you become.

~Jim Rohn~

Jim Rohn is one of my absolute favorites in the realm of personal development and motivation. He has a way of captivating an audience for hours, continuously delivering content after content after content. One of the things Jim Rohn said in his book, *The Power of Ambition* was, "If you come into a million dollars you'd better become a millionaire real fast." He said that if you don't grow to where your money is, your money will come down to where you are. What he's talking about is who you are at your core. It doesn't come from the materials that you gain. Your value comes from the person that you become while obtaining whatever you're seeking. Be careful when you're striving for success or to be in a certain place financially because you may reach the goal, but when you look back and see the person you've become to obtain that, you might not like it. But if you know in your heart that the object of your affection makes you better then that's where the value lies.

46

The Secret to happiness is freedom…
and the secret to freedom is courage.

~ Thucydides ~

Can I be honest? I want to be a millionaire. I want to live an abundant life. I want to be able to take my mom on a cruise, buy her a home, buy my dad the latest and greatest gadget for him to play with and treat him to a basketball game. I don't believe it's the wealth that will make me happy but it's the freedom that it brings that would make me happy. The freedom to be able to do and go anywhere I please excites me. To be free from debt and free from worry is a go for me. However, freedom comes at a price every free person must pay to be free. That price is courage. The courage to forge ahead despite setbacks, your background, your upbringing, and what everybody else is going to think of you. It takes courage to be an innovator. It takes courage to speak your own truth. It takes courage to do what's necessary instead of doing what's comfortable. It takes courage to be free.

47

It's a beautiful thing to know that we are in control of our thoughts. It's also a scary thing to know that our thoughts control our lives.

~Darren Mitchell~

We can't control the thoughts that enter our minds, but we can choose to entertain them or not. Most of us are dominated by disempowering thoughts. These thoughts lead to self-doubt. Fear. Make us anxious or nervous. Cause us to limit what we're capable of achieving. However, it's so wonderful to know that we don't have to entertain any of those thoughts. It feels good to know that with each passing thought I can allow it to pass by. I can consciously override the system (which is my brain) and tell it what I want to think. Now, it's also important to note that our thoughts dictate the actions that we take. The actions that we take lead to certain results. At the source of everything you received in your life is your thoughts. It's only scary if you allow negative thoughts to dominate your mind.

48

*A ship is always safe at shore
but that is not what it's built for.*

~Albert Einstein~

You are that ship. You will always be safe at home or in your tight little comfortable box. Where you are will not get you to where you want or need to be. Just because you're safe does not mean that is what you were built for. If we look to nature, we will see that everything grows to its maximum potential. Every plant, every tree, insect, or animal. We were created by the same Being. The Being that created nature, created us. We were built to reach our maximum potential. You were built to become! Leave that safe place, wherever it may be, and become who you are.

49

Confidence says, "I'm sure, but I could be wrong." Arrogance says, "I'm sure and I can't be wrong."

~Darren Mitchell~

I used to have this debate a lot about the difference between confidence and arrogance. So, I came up with my own definition. Here's the thing: an arrogant person cannot see the building crashing down around him. The arrogant person won't listen to wise counsel even when it's to his betterment. The confident person, on the other hand, is sure of herself. The confident person knows without a doubt but still leaves open the possibility for error. The subtle difference between confidence and arrogance is that confidence allows the space to be wrong and is OK with that. Arrogance leaves no room for error, no space to be wrong, and can only see things from its own perspective.

50

Done is better than perfect.

~DeBora Ricks~

Just get it done! Do you think successful people wait until everything is perfect to get started? Do you think they wait until all the stars have aligned to move forward? No, successful people get started, get things done, and improve along the way. That's the way it's always been done. Success leaves clues. I could edit this book 100 times wanting it to be perfect or I can finish it first and worry about it later. I decided on the latter.

51

Being ignorant is not so much a shame,
as being unwilling to learn.

~Benjamin Franklin~

Ignorance is a part of growth. It's a part of life. What do I mean? We're born not knowing a thing. Our minds are like sponges, absorbing everything that enters our ears, eyes, noses, and the rest of our senses. However, our young brains don't know how to interpret the many bits of information entering our senses. We need the help of others in order to interrupt it all. This is the beginning of ignorance. To be ignorant is to simply not know. There's no shame in that. Ignorance is the first stage of learning. The shame comes from being unwilling to learn. Where there's no learning, there's no growth and we were all put on this planet to grow. The moment we stop growing we start dying. Never stop learning.

52

Sometimes burdens are placed on us to show others how to overcome them.

~Darren Mitchell~

I've had hurdles sprinkled throughout my entire life. Some took me out for a short period; some took me out for a while. I always questioned them. I wondered to myself, "Why me? Why do I have to go through this? What did I do to deserve this?" Have you ever considered that maybe you're going through what you're going through because you're strong enough to handle it and you need to show someone who isn't how to overcome their burdens? Turn your trials into testimonies.

53

The only person you are destined to become is the person you decide to be.

~Ralph Waldo Emerson~

Life is determined by the decisions you make. Everything about you is a choice. I don't subscribe to any fixed way of being, even though we may be born with certain tendencies. This means we may tend to do a certain thing in each situation, however, we have the conscious power to choose to do something different. Therefore, the person you are destined to become is a decision you must make. It does not matter about your environment or family history. We all know people that come from the worst of the worst environments that pushed through. We all know or have heard of someone who grew up without parents but somehow overcame every obstacle to become a success. That's because who you are is a choice.

54

You gotta stop watering dead plants.

~ Unknown ~

This quote makes me think about all the dead relationships and dead people I used to have in my life. Watering things or people who are dead is simply pointless and wasteful. Think about it; all that water you're using on a dead relationship or dead people in your life could be poured into someone who is thirsty for what you have to offer. Believe it or not, there are people that exist who would love to receive what you must give. Unfortunately, you'll never reach those people because you're too busy wasting your water on dead plants. A dead plant can do nothing but zap unnecessary energy from you. Identify the dead plants in your life and then do yourself a favor and get rid of them.

55

If you aren't willing to work for it,
don't complain about not having it.

~ Toby McKeehan ~

Many issues people face would be taken care of if we learned to accept responsibility for where we are. You have what you have because you have done certain actions that lead to a result. What am I saying? Your life is a result of your actions. That's a very hard pill to swallow. It's much easier to blame and complain. To blame the times we live in, to blame the government or our parents. To complain that we weren't given the same chances as others to succeed. To complain that you don't have enough or simply aren't enough. However, I believe life is about two things: what you want and what you're willing to do to obtain it. Whenever you're not willing to do the things necessary to get what you want, what do people often do? Complain. Guess what? If you were doing the necessary things to get what you want, there wouldn't be a need to complain.

56

Sometimes the fear won't go away,
so you'll have to do it afraid.

~ Unknown ~

You will face many life-changing moments that will scare the pants off you. These are moments so big they could potentially alter the course of your life. Do you miss an opportunity of a lifetime or do you boldly step forth despite the fear? I'm part of Toastmasters International. Toastmasters is an organization designed to help individuals overcome their fear of public speaking or just become better speakers. One year, I took on the role as president of my club. Each week I stood up to face my audience and nerves would completely overtake me. Here's the funny part, the nervousness NEVER went away! What I learned was how to manage my fear. I learned how to channel it. Because what I learned through research is that your body processes fear and excitement in the same way. So, that's what I did instead. I got excited each week! I got pumped up before I went on stage and it was the best experience of my life.

57

*Life is a dance between making
it happen and letting it happen.*

~Arianna Huffington~

Often in life, you'll have to get accustomed to making things happen. What's equally important is learning what's inside of your control and what's outside of your control. Think about it this way. If you want a new job, you must grind the pavement or, to use more modern terminology, the computer. You must get off your butt and submit hundreds of applications. That's called making it happen. Letting it happen comes *after* making it happen. In other words, letting it happen is a result of making it happen. After you've filled out countless applications and even followed up with each, what happens next is outside of your control. Once you master making and letting things happen, it then becomes a dance. There's no longer a struggle because you know and trust the process.

58

Winners never lose.

~Gerri Bohanan~

Have you ever lost in a competition and still felt good afterward? I remember the time I competed in the Toastmasters International Speech Contest. I made it past the club, area, and district levels. In the division, I lost without even placing third. It was a hard loss for me. However, I remember my friend Tyrone saying, "Just remember what Gerri says, 'winners never lose.'" At that moment, I realized that winning was a state of mind. It isn't determined by a panel of judges who are just as imperfect of a creature as I am. In fact, if you really pay attention, most judges can't come close to doing things you're doing anyway. So, who are they to even decide who wins or who loses? Winners *NEVER* lose!

59

*Anything or anyone that does not
bring you alive is too small for you.*

~ David Whyte ~

Who are you surrounding yourself with? Have you considered that the reason you keep doubting yourself is because that's what you've heard your entire life, and somewhere along the way you decided to believe it? Have you considered that the reason you haven't elevated yourself to new heights is because every time you present an idea to your friends they shoot it down? How long can you live like that? Suppressing the inner giant that desperately needs to be released for you to truly come alive and show the world who you are will only lead to anger, resentment, and eventually depression. Therefore, it is so important to be around people who help bring you alive. Who *want* to see you alive? Life is too short to accept anything less.

60

If I had asked people what they wanted,
they would have said faster horses.

~ Henry Ford ~

To me, this quote means that sometimes you just have to follow your own heart, no matter what people think. I know it's good to do your research first and put feelers out there to get an idea of what people want, but what if your idea is so revolutionary that people don't even realize it's your product or service that they really want? That would take an enormous amount of faith and courage and may be even a little crazy but that's OK. I believe some of the most famous revolutionaries in history had to be a little crazy to achieve the great things they did. Think about it, 50 years ago who would have thought we could have hot food in less than two minutes, send messages through the airwaves, store all the world's information in your hand, and get news instantaneously through something called social media? The point is to not worry about what people are saying. What's important is what your heart is saying.

61

Not every day is a good day.
Show up anyway.

~Gymaholic~

Every gym enthusiast out there knows all too well how true this saying is. Although the pros make it look easy, trust me that every day will not be a good day. If you're alive, nothing will always be good. Your spouse won't always be the nicest person in the world. The children won't always be on their best behavior. You won't always feel like doing the things on your to-do-list. But the one difference between high achievers and underachievers is that high achievers show up anyway. I can say with confidence that I don't always feel motivated or inspired to show up. The most prolific writers and painters of antiquity all gave the same advice on inspiration. That it's a load of crap. Excuse my technical language. But what they're saying is if you relied solely on inspiration you'd never accomplish anything. Do you know where inspiration will undoubtedly always come from? Action. Yes, sometimes you get inspired to act but that happens so infrequently that only a fool would rely on it. Inspiration comes from showing up day in and day out no matter what.

62

We are what we repeatedly do.
Excellence, then, is not an act, but a habit.

~Aristotle~

This is extremely difficult for many to grasp. The fact that we are what we repeatedly do says underneath that who and what we are is our fault. That what we have and what we've become are essentially our own doing. Therefore, set a target. And don't let that target be something weak or mediocre. Aim high enough to stretch yourself. Focus on excellence! Excellence is defined as a way of being that is extraordinary. Man, I love that. However, what I find interesting is that a synonym for excellence is the word distinction. It is a separation from things or people. To focus on the things that set you apart from everyone else is to focus on excellence. However, these things must be done repeatedly for them to take root in your character.

63

Take time today to just…be.

~Darren Mitchell~

If you're like me, your mind races at a thousand miles per minute. If this is coupled with always being on the run, you have a recipe for burnout. Before I learned to develop healthy boundaries around my time and energy, I used to experience burnout all the time. What I learned from those experiences is that it is OK to take time to just be. Not do, not try, not strive, but just be. Most people in today's society, including myself at times, have an unhealthy relationship with time. We think there is never enough time to do the things we need to. It was only when I realized that the only difference between me and the people I look up to is how we spend our time. I realized that there was plenty of time to do everything. The question is are you spending your time on things that truly *MATTER*?

64

Just because my path is different

doesn't mean I'm Lost.

~ Unknown ~

I believe this judgment is placed on many of us from our parents. I have an understanding now that parents mean well when raising us. They only want the best for us. However, the best for us is how they see it. No one, not even your parents, can truly know what's best for you. Only you can know that. So, when you decide to take a path that they aren't in agreement with, they may be inclined to say you're lost. Each of us on this journey called life must choose his/her own path. However, just because mine or yours is different from someone else's does not mean we're lost.

65

When you shift your mind from 'I win' to
'We all win,' that's the moment
true change can happen.

~Darren Mitchell~

We are all selfish creatures. I get it. Everyone is concerned about their own self-interest. But it is those special people who can step outside of themselves and concern themselves with the self-interest of others who make the most impact. These are the people who do not see themselves as individuals but as a conscious collective. They are people who understand that what they do always affects someone else. This is at the root of shifting your mind from 'I win' to 'we all win'. I had to recognize that in my job, church, and the other organizations I was a part of that I had a direct impact on those who were a part of the same thing. If I was late to work, someone else had to cover me until I got in. This meant they would not only have to carry their own load but mine as well. The selfish individual doesn't see the impact they have on their group and is solely concerned with self. The moment you step outside of yourself is where transformation exists.

66

*A river cuts through a rock not because
of its power but because of its persistence.*

~ Unknown ~

We often think that it's only through the use of force that we knock things over. If we try something and it doesn't work, our mind tells us we didn't try hard enough. If we ask for something and we are told no, then we may think we should have used a firmer tone and walk away defeated. However, if we look at the formation of one of the seven wonders of the world, the Grand Canyon, we see that it wasn't power that formed it. The Grand Canyon wasn't formed by an asteroid striking the plant but by running water over millions of years. It is persistence that carves our path to success. Continuing day in and day out without fail leads to victory. Victory doesn't come to the person who is the strongest. Victories come to the persistent.

67

*A truly strong person does not need
the approval of others any more than
a lion needs the approval of sheep.*

~ Vernon Howard ~

Think about it. A lion, the king of the jungle as he's known, has no natural predators. A lion walks around with its head held high. His only worry is where his next meal might come from. And even then, he has nothing to worry about because he isn't even the one doing the hunting. Now, why in the world would a lion, with all his might, need to seek the approval of a sheep? Sheep aren't the hunter but the hunted. They have no teeth to fight with or tough skin to defend. It's fair to say that the sheep are much weaker animals in comparison to lions. So why would you, in all your might need to seek the approval of others? Unless you view yourself as weak as a helpless sheep, you don't need the approval of others. The question to ask yourself in any given situation is, "Who am I?" Do you see yourself as a sheep? Or are you a lion?

68

It's not what happens to you.
It's what you do about it.

~ W. Mitchell ~

I remember one day going outside to my car and finding the door was cracked open slightly. As I peered into the window suspiciously, I noticed the inside had been ransacked. Papers were everywhere, my glove box was wide open, and the center console had been rummaged through. To make matters worse, I looked inside the trunk and my duffle bag was missing. What made that so bad was my favorite workout pants and cologne were in the bag. Now, I could have freaked out and flown into a fit of rage (and I did, by the way, ha-ha!), however, after I regained my composure I remembered a famous quote from W. Mitchell who said, "In life, it's not what happens to you, it's what you do about it." I immediately said to myself, "OK, Darren, your car has been broken into, now what are you going to do about it?" Here's what's interesting about asking what you can do about a situation: your brain begins to search for solutions. Thank God, I had the money to replace the bag, cologne, and pants so that's what I did. Because guess what, life will happen to you. However, that's not what life is about. It's about what you will do about it.

69

*People often say that motivation doesn't last.
Well, neither does bathing — that's why we
recommend it daily.*

-Zig Ziglar-

Speaker, trainer, and author Brendon Burchard says that we are like power plants. A power plant doesn't have energy, it generates it. When you see yourself this way, you know then that you can't find motivation and it must be generated from within. Motivation doesn't happen to you. It happens because of you. Motivation is a fleeting thing. You will hardly ever feel motivated. Motivation comes because of doing the thing that needs to get done. Just like the power plant example, it is the spinning of turbines that generate the energy a power plant produces. Again, it is the action. Do you want motivation? Get into action every single day.

70

The best way to predict the

future is to create it.

~Abraham Lincoln~

I will always be big on taking responsibility for your own life. I don't care how you were raised. What conditions you were brought up in. If you grew up with two parents, one, or none at all. The power to change your future will always be in your hands. Do you want to know how your future will turn out? Create it right now. Stop waiting for a fairy godparent to appear and rescue you out of your situation or circumstances. Stop expecting someone to find you and save you. News flash! No one is coming. So, now what? Now, you fight. Now, you create. Don't believe me? Well, guess what? You're creating right now, whether you're consciously aware of it or not. Everything you have in your life now is a result of the life you chose to create. Of course, there are things that are truly outside of your control. But what's always in your control is your reaction to it. And it is that reaction that creates your reality and thus creates your future.

71

Certain things catch your eye but pursue
only those that capture the heart.

~Ancient Indian Proverb~

I'm truly beginning to understand the concept of this quote. I believe that 90 percent of people in the world focus on things that are unimportant. But here's what's interesting: the most unimportant things tend to be the most attractive. The reason why we focus on them is because they catch the eye and they offer immediate gratification to a person who is starving for happiness. At our core, we all are striving for happiness in everything we do, from raising our children right to making more money, having a spouse, or even the clothes that we buy. On some level, every action we take is because we think it will either give us immediate happiness or lead to happiness. On the flipside, the things that truly matter and capture our heart usually take something from us. There's always a tradeoff of some kind where we must give up something. To pursue a healthy body will cost you time, energy, and effort. To pursue wealth will cost friends, family, time, and discipline. To pursue meaningful relationships, you will have to give up grudges and resentment. All these things may cost us time and own ego, but these are the things that really matter in life. So, stop reaching for the low hanging fruit that catches the eye. Instead, pursue the things that may seem difficult at first, but in the end, leave you feeling the most fulfilled.

72

What you remove from your life is
often more valuable than what you add.

~Darren Mitchell~

I often hear people complain about how life is so depressing and miserable. Most complaints are centered around three things: love, money, or happiness. Single people are angry that they can't find anyone, and married people are angry because they married the wrong person. Rich people complain that they don't have meaningful relationships and are always questioning what their true purpose is in life. Poor people complain there's never enough money and rich people are taking it all. What I have found in my journey in life is that it's the clearing and removing of the shrubs that make a way for everything I want to enter my life. When money was an issue, I found that removing myself from my current job (not before finding a new one of course) made a way for more money to enter. When I felt like no one in my circle of friends was headed in the same direction I was, I decided there was no need to complain or belittle them. They were who they were and there was nothing wrong with them, however, I needed to clear them from my life in a way that they no longer had influence over me. Alcohol was another monster that wreaked havoc in my life. Once I removed it, my life took off like a rocket ship. So, I ask you, what things in your life are you lugging around that are preventing you from being your best self?

73

If you are depressed, you are living in the past.

If you are anxious, you are living in the future.

If you are at peace, you are living in the present.

~Lao Tzu~

Every spiritual teacher will tell you that the ultimate state of awareness is to be fully present. How do you know if you're being fully present? There's a sense of calmness and peace that overtakes you. Most of the time we use our minds to stay stuck either in the past or the future. We're sad or even feel guilty when we constantly worry about something that either happened to us or happened because of us in the past, no matter how distant. In fact, we think it is somehow noble of us to carry the guilt of some wrong we have done in the past. We have anxiety when we use our minds to worry about some future event that hasn't even happened yet. The first thing to remember is that the past and the future are both illusions that we create and make real in our own minds. I want you to realize that there is no power for you in making the past real. There is no power in a guilty mind. There is also no power in a worry-filled mind. The only real power comes from handling what's in front of you in the present moment. I want you to ask this question anytime you find yourself stuck in the past or future: "Is this happening to me right now?"

74

*Don't wait for everything to be perfect
before you decide to live your life.*

~Joyce Meyer~

Make mistakes! Sorry to start by screaming at you, but we are too afraid to make mistakes. To fail. To hit our heads. To fall. To look stupid in front of everybody. To look like a failure. Do you know the real reason why you want everything to be perfect before you act on something? You're afraid of how it will look to other people if you do something and you're not perfect at it. And if that's not it, the only other reason is that you're afraid that you aren't capable of bouncing back from a failure or loss. Do you know what one quality of the super successful is? That they see themselves as being able to accomplish anything, no matter the obstacle standing in their way? Stop waiting for perfect, it's not real. Life begins when you decide to start living.

75

A secret to happiness is letting every situation be what it is, instead of what you think it should be.

~Unknown~

So many people operate in the false world of what should be. First, let's be clear, "should" doesn't exist. You can't do anything with should. Should only leads to sadness and frustration. If you are always thinking about what should be, this means you're never satisfied with what is. I'm not saying you must agree with what is, but I love to look at things from a power perspective, as in what will give me the most power. That starts with accepting what is. Once you accept things the way they are, you can choose to do something to change it or leave it how it is. Remember, everything is already exactly how it should be or else it wouldn't be. You are where you should be. The world is where it should be. Once we accept this, then we can choose a different reality. You may then say, "Well, what about accepting people?" I'm glad you asked. My mother, whom I love dearly, used to get on my nerves! But I realized when I got older, this was because I wanted her to be different than who she was, and I was trying to change her into who I thought she should be. Oddly enough, I didn't see her differently until I accepted her for who she was. For anyone who has trouble with a close friend or family member, try repeating this, "I accept [insert person's name] for who they are AND who they are not."

76

*It's in your darkest moments where
you discover your brightest ideas.*

~Darren Mitchell~

In a life of comfort and ease, most people never achieve what they set out to do. Most people, if their basic needs are being met, never push themselves to their optimum potential. Look at children who are born with a silver spoon in their mouth, they never come to appreciate the value of hard work, persistence, and failure. However, take a person who comes from nothing and watch them achieve the impossible. Think about your own life. It was those times of deepest despair that you gained your greatest triumph. It's when your back is up against the wall and when your deadline is tomorrow that you suddenly come alive. Don't run from the dark moments but see the blessing in them.

77

We must all suffer from one of two pains:
the pain of discipline or the pain of regret.
The difference is discipline weighs ounces
while regret weighs tons.

~Jim Rohn~

Life is tough. I'll say it again: life is tough. We all struggle to eat right, be the best person we can be, maintain healthy relationships with loved ones, and be financially independent. All of which are very, very painful. However, here's the thing: doing the opposite in hindsight is always more painful. We think about how we need to work out more, but when we think about how much is involved or what needs to be sacrificed, we quit. We think about how we need to spend more time with our families, but then "life" gets in the way and we don't. However, the pain of regret will be enormous when we've gained 20 lbs. by not working out and eating healthy. Worse still, we may develop a disease or condition because of our poor lifestyle or the loved one we said we would visit one day, could pass away. Wow, how painful is that? I'll tell you it's a lot more painful than disciplining yourself to allot special time on your calendar on a weekly or monthly basis to see family and friends. Getting a disease that is lifestyle related is more painful than disciplining yourself to eat healthy and workout. Ultimately, you have two options in life: pay now and play later or play now and pay later. The choice is yours.

78

Being alone is determined by who's around you.
Being lonely is determined by what's in you.

~Darren Mitchell~

We all are alone at times. Some are more alone than others are, of course. However, I believe we never have to feel lonely. One of the biggest lessons I have learned in life is to enjoy my own company. There's nothing wrong with being around people, but always needing to be around others could be a strong indicator that you are avoiding yourself. The more I accepted myself, the more I became OK with just me. When I was able to educate myself, entertain myself, and explore the world by myself I felt less lonely. It's interesting looking back to when I *had* to be the center of attention because it made me feel better about Darren. Now, if I'm the center of attention it's because I'm sharing myself with others. This is not from fear of being alone, but from the love I have of myself to give to others. The first way, I go home feeling empty and inadequate. The second way, I go home feeling powerful and fulfilled. The latter is the same feeling I carry with me when I'm alone.

79

If you would have your son to walk honorably through the world, you must not attempt to clear the stones from his path but teach him to walk firmly over them - not insist upon leading him by the hand but let him learn to go alone.

~Anne Bronte~

One important lesson I've learned in my adulthood has to do with my childhood. A parent's sole purpose in the life of their child is to prepare them for independence and to give them the tools necessary to survive without them. Every species on the planet, in different ways, of course, prepares their children for the world. Only humans, because of fear, want to remove every stone from a child's path. This thinking stems from the belief that you're helping the child, when, in fact, you're only robbing them of their independence. Instead, teach your child how to deal with life's stones. Impart your wisdom to the child but allow them to learn on their own.

80

When I think about who I am vs.
Who I could be. It scares me.

~Darren Mitchell~

Who reading this book can honestly say that they are living life to their full potential? I would assume that 99 percent would say no. That would mean on some level, you know exactly what you're capable of accomplishing. However, for whatever reason, you aren't living up to that. You are aware of where you are, but you're frustrated because you know that you could be further along than you are. It frightens me when the vision of who I REALLY am enters my mind. Why? Because I know at a very conscious level that the only thing that is stopping me is fear. It's fear itself that scares me. However, we know fear isn't real, right? Ninety-five percent of the things we fear never actually manifest. So what's stopping you? Imagine the person you could be and simply be that.

81

The greatest discovery of any generation is that human beings can alter their lives by altering the attitudes of their minds.

-Albert Schweitzer-

This is such a profound statement that many have spoken on, but few apply to their lives. Much, not ALL, of what we experience is simply because of our attitude towards it. Think about those rough periods in your life when you may have been sad, anxious, or even depressed. What is it that causes you to get out of the slump you're in? Well, one day you wake up and decide no more. It's simply a change in attitude. Nothing outside of you changes. But for whatever reason, something inside of you changes and you begin to look at your life in a new light. Your perspective changes. When you're depressed, you think there's no way out of this situation, so you never attempt to find one. Your actions always follow your mindset. However, the moment your attitude changes, you begin to move different, see different and be different. Opportunities that have been there the whole time become clear to you. Every human being has the power to some degree to change their circumstances by changing their attitude.

82

A leader is best when people barely know he exists, when his work is done, his aim fulfilled, they will say: we did it ourselves.

~ Lao Tzu ~

This is such an empowering quote because when we typically think of a leader we think of someone who is out in the forefront. Someone who wants to be seen and heard. A person who wants everyone to know he/she is the one in charge. However, more importantly, this leader wants to take full credit for any success under their leadership. However, the best leaders lead in a more covert manner. They don't seek recognition or notoriety. Their only concern is the success of the people they're leading. The best leaders don't bark orders and demand their will to be done. Why expend that much energy only to have everyone hate you in the end anyway? Great leaders lead in a way that inspires and empowers others to lead. This way once the job is complete they'll think they did it themselves. Meanwhile, you as the leader can give yourself a quiet and humble pat on the back.

83

You will never do anything in this world without courage. It is the greatest quality of the mind next to honor.

~Aristotle~

Ahh, courage. I could write an entire book on courage alone. Courage is the one quality that if you had nothing else, somehow you would manage to succeed in whatever you want in life. Many people think its competence, including myself at times, that puts you on the path of success. That if I only *knew* more I would be successful. So, what do we do? We watch hours upon hours of YouTube videos. We read countless books and listen to endless audios. However, let me ask you a question. If any of you have been skydiving, and even if you haven't, when you're standing on the edge waiting to jump, is it competence or is it courage that ultimately gets you out there? Even the experienced skydiver who has logged thousands of jumps knows on some level that any jump could be their last. So, what is it that causes them to take that leap of faith? It's simple: courage. So, if there's any quality worth building, worth honing, and worth mastering, its courage. But here's the thing: courage cannot be studied to be mastered. It must be practiced.

84

Happiness is a choice. You can choose to be happy. There's going to be stress in life, but it's your choice whether you let it affect you or not."

- Valerie Bertinelli -

Not only is happiness a choice, but everything is a choice. We make the mistake of allowing ourselves to be victims and thinking we must do or feel a certain way in certain situations. If your house burned to the ground one day in a random freak accident, how would you feel? Most people think you're supposed to be angry, sad or depressed. What I'm saying is that even if you came home to a burned-down house, you can still choose how you want to feel about it. The question is, why is it so important to choose your feelings? Because there are certain feelings that are optimal to your daily performance. It's all about being powerful in the world. Feelings such as sadness and fear can cause you to become weak and closed off from the world. However, feelings of joy and confidence allow you to show up as your highest self. What better way to handle a stressful situation than powerfully and with a confident I-can-do-anything smile?

85

There is only one way to avoid criticism:
do nothing, say nothing, and be nothing.

~Aristotle~

Fear of criticism or the fear of judgment is the greatest fear of all. Yes, it's even greater than public speaking. Why, you ask? Well, behind the fear of public speaking is the fear of judgment. In fact, most fears can be traced back to a fear of judgment. Some people will say, "I don't want to start a business because I might fail." So, you ask, "You're afraid of failure, right?" Wrong! You aren't afraid to fail. What you're really afraid of is LOOKING like a failure. You're afraid that people will judge you as a failure. It's the same thing that happens when we do something embarrassing. It's only embarrassing if people are around to see it. So, if you never want to be judged or you want to avoid criticism at all costs, the only way to do this is by doing absolutely nothing. However, I would suggest becoming numb to judgment and criticism altogether. Once this happens, there is nothing on this planet you can't do.

86

I hope that in this year to come, you make mistakes. Because if you are making mistakes, then you are making new things, trying new things, learning, living, pushing yourself, changing yourself, changing your world. You're doing things you've never done before, and more importantly, you're doing something."

~Neil Gaiman~

On some conscious level, we all know that the only way we grow is through trial and error even if we don't want to go through the process. Really pay attention to what Neil Gaiman is saying in this quote: "Because if you are making mistakes, then you are making new things, trying new things…" He is saying we should begin to see the blessings mistakes bring such as new opportunities, new experiences, and chances to learn and grow. Wow, if we could only replace those thoughts of fear and doubt with, "I wonder what I'm going to learn from this experience?" or, "What's the blessing in this?" There's something special to be said about those people who learn to push themselves beyond their own limits.

87

Feeling gratitude and not expressing it is like wrapping a present and not giving it.

~ William Arthur Ward ~

Do you remember getting super excited the night before Christmas? Maybe you still do. You would sit on the floor with presents, gift-wrap paper, and tape with the house in disarray, as if a tornado had touched down in the living room. But you don't care as the only thing on your mind is the joy that will be on the faces of the people you'll be handing your gifts to. Imagine the excitement you go through the night before Christmas, delightfully wrapping up presents only to change your mind and decide to keep every last one. Having gratitude in your heart but not giving it is the same. Are there people in your life you're grateful for? I bet you they don't know how much they mean to you. Your gratitude is a gift. And, unlike physical presents, gratitude never runs out. There isn't a limit to how much gratitude you have in your heart. Gratitude is the gift that just keeps on giving. So, go tell someone how much you care, how thankful you are for them in your life. I promise you the happiness it will bring is priceless.

88

People with clear, written goals, accomplish far more in a shorter period of time than people without them could ever imagine.

~Brian Tracy~

I know you've heard this one time and time again. But have you honestly used it? Have you sat down to think about what you really want in life? OK, I get it, you may get stuck on this part so let me help you out. I want you to imagine your own funeral. Yes, think about your own death. What are the things you think you want to have accomplished for people to say that you had lived a fulfilled life? Everything that you want to accomplish before death is a goal. Write it down this instant and be crystal clear about it. Write down every detail of where you are, what you're wearing, and most importantly how you feel. Because study after study has shown that those who write down their goals are more likely to succeed in life than those who do not.

89

Running away from any problem only increases the distance from the solution. The easiest way to escape from the problem is to solve it.

~ Unknown ~

The way I see it is that the longer you run away from a problem, the further you push it into the future. Moreover, the problem often doubles when you deal with it later. If any of you reading this have ever had the pleasure of getting any sort of parking ticket or citation in Washington D.C., you know all too well what happens when you put off paying it. The ticket doubles in 30 days if it is not paid. A ticket that would have originally cost you $150, which is a significant amount of money by the way, can easily wind up costing you $300 if you do not pay within the due period. Life can be the same. We get bills and letters in the mail and sometimes think if we ignore them that they'll magically go away. But do they? No, of course not. In fact, most of those letters or bills have a penalty for not responding right away. We must attack our problems in life the same way we need to attack those bills – right away and head on. The only way to handle a problem is to act on it. So, what are you waiting for?

90

We are taught you must blame your father, your sisters, your brothers, the school, the teachers - but never blame yourself. It's never your fault. But it's always your fault, because if you wanted to change you're the one who has got to change.

~Katharine Hepburn~

I must say that the moment I ran across this quote it became an instant favorite. I used to blame everyone and everything for the problems I was experiencing. I blamed my mom for not being nurturing enough. I blamed my dad for being too hard on me as a kid. I blamed the judicial system for putting me in jail. But you know what happens when you blame anyone but yourself for where you are in life? You put the power in someone else's hands to change the trajectory of your life. When you blame someone else you're saying, "Hey, my life won't change until someone else changes it." Is that what you really want? Well, unfortunately, even if that is what you want, life just doesn't work that way. You must look at your life as if everything in it is your fault. In addition, if there is anything that you are unsatisfied with then you and only you must change it.

91

Inaction breeds doubt and fear. Action breeds confidence and courage. If you want to conquer fear, do not sit home and think about it. Go out and get busy.

~Dale Carnegie~

As I sit here writing this book, I realize more and more how important getting into action really is. For some reason, everything seems larger than what it really is if you're thinking about it. This is how your mind keeps you "safe." Your mind doesn't know that it isn't living in times of old when fear was needed constantly to keep you safe from *real* danger. Your mind believes it is helping you by making things seem bigger than they are. However, you, the being behind your thoughts, must know better. Do you know how to see things for what they really are? Take action. Stop daydreaming about what it could be and go see it for yourself. Stop thinking your mind knows better than what experience can tell you. Do what Dale says: go out and get busy!

92

When you doubt your power,
you give power to your doubt.

~ Honore del Balzac ~

This quote made me realize that our true power lies in what we focus on. I was in the gym one morning about to squat a weight I had never done before. I had never enjoyed working on my legs, so I had neglected them. Because of this, they were the weakest part of my body. Recently, I began to change that by consistently working out on "leg day." Now, because I've always had in the back of my mind that my legs were weak, I wouldn't challenge myself as I often did on other exercises. When the time came to set a personal record, I doubted my ability to do it. As I held the weight on top of my shoulders and began the descent downward, the pressure scared me, and I immediately came back up. My gym partner and mentor looked at me and said, "Your legs are stronger than you think." At that moment, I decided not to focus on what I thought I couldn't do but to shift focus on what I could do. The instant I stopped doubting myself I was able to successfully set a personal record in my squat exercise. Nothing about me changed physically. I just chose to give power to my power and not to my doubts.

93

A pessimist sees the difficulty in every opportunity; an optimist sees the opportunity in every difficulty.

~ Winston Churchill~

Do you have a secret pessimist running the show in your mind? If you're anything like me the answer is a resounding YES! Every time I think about a new video to post on social media or get offered a speaking opportunity, my inner pessimist pops up. It's funny how he only pops up when there's something your heart really wants to do. The person you ultimately become is determined by the voice you listen to the most. There's an optimist inside all of us who dares to dream big and knows that one day the dream will become a reality. The optimist doesn't see obstacles but challenges. It may take something from us, but challenges can be won. Life will be forever filled with challenges and difficulties. Life will also be forever filled with opportunities. More importantly, life is about perspective. How you see the world will determine who you are in the world. How you see the world is decided by who's running the show in your mind. So, will you decide to see the opportunity in every difficulty or the difficulty in every opportunity?

94

He who asks a question remains a fool for five minutes; he who does not ask a question remains a fool forever.

~Chinese proverb~

Do you know that children are the smartest people on the planet? As adults, we are often too proud to ask questions, even at times when we should ask the most. Not a child though. A child is so curious about life that they will ask why until you as the "all knowing" parent can no longer answer, so you say, "because it is, now leave it alone!" Did you also know the geniuses of the world are just like children? They're curious. They have a burning desire to answer life's most difficult questions. And they never stop asking them. Like a child who continually asks the question why, so does the genius. But here's the thing: a genius is only a genius because they know that they know nothing. A fool is a fool because he thinks he knows everything.

95

A wise man never knows all,
only fools know everything.

~African Proverb~

The most famous words spoken by every young person in the world are, "I know." However, it is adults too that are guilty of uttering these debilitating words. Why do I call them debilitating? Because once you say, "I know" you cut off any information from entering your brain. The more you say "I know" the less you learn. Only a fool would think they knew everything. Once you know everything, there's nothing else to be gained. A wise person admits they know nothing. He or she knows that if you listen to no one or read nothing, then you'll always know what you already know. Therefore, the Bible says to keep a childlike mind. A child constantly asks questions, is always curious, and wants to know more. This is the way of the wise.

96

Don't try to be like someone else.
Find out who you are and be that.

~ Unknown ~

With the advent of social media, we as people have become connected in ways never thought possible. Because of this connection, it has become easier to peer into the lives of those we admire. Seeing how masterfully they perform their prospective craft or even how successful they are creating a desire to imitate who they are. But here's the thing: you can never be them. It's biologically impossible. They are who they are, and you are who you are. So why try to be like someone else? The world doesn't need another them. Trust me, one is enough. What the world desperately needs is you. The REAL you. The you behind everything you're trying to hide. Once you discover who that is, just be that.

97

Ego says, 'Once everything falls into place then I'll feel peace.' Spirit says, 'Find your peace, and then everything will fall into place.'

~Marianne Williamson~

Ask 10 people what the ego is, and you'll get 10 different answers. I like to think of the ego as the part of you that will stop at nothing to "protect" you. It will do whatever it can to please itself. The ego will even lie to get what it wants. I believe the Bible describes the ego as the "flesh." The flesh needs to feel pleasure to have peace. Given those terms, your peace then is always fleeting. Things will never fall into place because the ego is only satisfied with temporary things. Do you know why the spirit says to find your peace first? Because the spirit knows that everything is already in the right place. There's no need to fix or wait for it. If you understand how God and the universe work, you know that everything is exactly where it is supposed to be. That is where you find peace: in knowing that everything is exactly as it should be.

98

You only lose what you cling to.

~ Buddha ~

One of the seven spiritual laws of success outlined in the book of the same name by Deepak Chopra is the law of attachment. What Deepak so eloquently explains is that there are an infinite number of outcomes to everything in life. When you become attached to one outcome, it is easy for sadness, disappointment, and even depression to set in. Why? Because when something doesn't go the way we expect it to, it is a serious blow to our ego. You're disappointed when you lose a job if you're attached to that specific job being your only means of income. Here's how this quote goes even deeper. What if you never saw that job as being yours in the first place? Can you ever lose it? If your friend loses their keys, do you get stressed out? No. Why? Because they didn't belong to you. What we deem as ours we tend to cling to. We take possession of it. Once it's lost it's as if you've lost a part of yourself. But once we're able to detach ourselves from this physical world, only then can we become free.

99

When I accept myself, I am freed from the burden of needing you to accept me.

~Dr. Steve Maraboli~

I remember it like it was yesterday. I had an interview for a job that I wanted badly. I had been in a dead-end job for two years and I had finally mustered the courage to leave. The day of the interview, I woke up early to pray and meditate for an entire hour. Through that experience, it was revealed to me that true love is acceptance and I needed to truly love myself by accepting everything I was and everything I was not. At that moment, I realized I didn't need to study anything or try to sound impressive to my future employer. All I needed to do was be myself. When I went into that interview, I went in with a Superman level of confidence. I was truly free that day because I said to myself, "If I'm not good enough for this position then this position isn't for me." Well, guess what? I got the job! So, please free yourself from the burden of needing anybody to accept you. The only person who needs to accept you is you.

100

Be selective with your battles.
Sometimes peace is better than being right.

~ Unknown ~

Before every battle we face in life, it's important to weigh the costs. There are always costs associated with battle. Living in America in 2018, most of the battles we face aren't physical or natural but more mental. They are battles of the mind and ego with one another. Unfortunately, we as humans are so concerned and even blinded by the need to be right that we lose sight of what's important. We get into heated debates and arguments with friends and family and sometimes lose them in the process. For what? To be right? You may gain a notch under your I-was-right belt; however, a trusted friend is gone forever. Was it worth it? Would it have cost you as much to keep quiet and keep the peace as well? Probably not. So, learn to choose your battles wisely.

101

*The source of all frustration is non-acceptance.
If you are experiencing any negative emotion,
ask yourself this question: 'What am I not
accepting about this situation?'*

~Darren Mitchell~

I used to ask, "Why me? Why do I have to go through pain and suffering? Why does tragedy happen?" However, once I came to an understanding, I started to see the beauty in all my dark moments. Human beings have a very dichotomous experience in that everything is known because we compare it to what it's not. We know light because it is not dark. We know right because of left. Therefore, as of right now in the evolutionary phase (and I mean in consciousness), we know of our bright moments because of the dark ones. I point this out so we can begin to see the blessing in all things. Imagine that you're on your way to work. Ten minutes into the drive, you run into stop and go traffic. Oh, and did I mention you were already running late? In an instant, you're furious, screaming at everyone in sight, and blowing the horn uncontrollably. Normally you would blame the traffic for "making" you mad, but traffic is what it is. and the moment that you accept this you can do something about it. Call your boss, tell her you're running late, and then use the time to listen to that new audiobook you purchased on Audible. The same principle can be applied to any situation. Just say to yourself, "I accept what is happening, now what can I do about it?"

Afterword

Let me say that this book took me much longer than it should have to write. However, I underestimated just how difficult it would be to write a book like this. I thought to myself, "It's just a book of quotes with a little explanation beside them. How hard could it be?" I originally gave myself two long months to complete the book. I got off to quite a great start. I told myself that I would finish 10 quotes a day and be finished in no time. It was an ambitious goal, but I knew that if I happened to fall off (which I did), it wouldn't hurt as much. However, I stuck to my original plan of 10 quotes per day for a grand total of two days. Then, after getting writer's block, I scaled my ambitious goal down to five quotes per day. After a week of that, I went a whole week without writing a single word. Then one week turned to two, then three, and finally I had all but given up on it. I soon realized that writing this little book was going to be a lot harder than expected. Because it was about 101 completely different topics at one time, it was much harder to get into a flow compared to if I was writing a chronological story. I decided to push the date of completion back an entire month. Then one month turned to two, which turned to three and finally I had enough. I set a final date and it took everything in me to stay on track. But I got it done and that's all that matters. What I learned, however, is that there will always be reasons for "why not" such as you're too busy, don't have the time, can't focus, whatever. But you must figure out the reasons why, and make it happen at all costs. I urge you, whatever unfinished business you have in your life, just get it done. Don't worry about dates or how long it has taken you. As Deborah Ricks put it, "Done is better than perfect."

55974166R00117

Made in the USA
Columbia, SC
20 April 2019